P9-DFK-825

AUG 1 3

LACROSSE

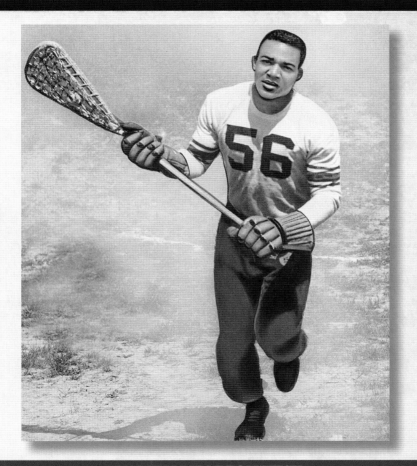

BY ANNABELLE TOMETICH

CONTENT CONSULTANT
JANE CLAYDON
LACROSSE HISTORIAN

Printed in the United States of America,
North Mankato, Minnesota
102011
012012

 THIS BOOK CONTAINS AT LEAST 10% RECYCLED MATERIALS.

Editor: Chrös McDougall
Copy Editor: Anna Comstock
Series Design and Cover Production: Craig Hinton
Interior Production: Kelsey Oseid

Photo Credits: Larry French/NCAA Photos/AP Images, cover (bottom), 41, 51, 54, 59 (bottom);
Amygdala Imagery/iStockphoto, cover (top); AP Images, 1, 45; Marilyn Angel Wynn/Getty Images, 5;
Nativestock Pictures/Photolibrary, 7; Itsuo Inouye/AP Images, 9; Bill Frakes/Sports Illustrated/Getty
Images, 13; North Wind Picture Archives, 15, 21, 58 (top); George Catlin/The Art Gallery Collection/
Alamy, 19; Bain News Service/Library of Congress, 23, 58 (middle); S&G/AP Images, 29, 58 (bottom);
J. A. Hampton/Getty Images, 33; John Ehlke/AP Images, 35; Rob Carr/AP Images, 42, 57, 59 (middle);
Robert E. Klein/ AP Images, 47, 59 (top); Jim Rogash/Getty Images, 49

Library of Congress Cataloging-in-Publication Data
Tometich, Annabelle, 1980-
 Lacrosse / by Annabelle Tometich.
     p. cm. -- (Best sport ever)
 Includes index.
 ISBN 978-1-61783-145-4
 1. Lacrosse--Juvenile literature. I. Title.
 GV989.14.T65 2012
 796.347--dc23
                              2011034460

TABLE of CONTENTS

CHAPTER 1

AN IDENTITY

Soon after Brett Bucktooth's son was born, he placed a small, wooden lacrosse stick on his baby's blanket. Bucktooth was an Iroquois. Like many Iroquois, his father had passed his love for lacrosse on to Bucktooth. Now Bucktooth wanted to pass the sport he loved on to his newborn son.

Lacrosse is much more than a game for the Iroquois. They have played lacrosse for hundreds of years. They believe the sport was a gift from their Creator. They play lacrosse to bring health to sick friends and to honor their ancestors. And many Iroquois have become quite good players.

Bucktooth is a midfielder for the Iroquois Nationals. One of his teammates is attacker Gewas Schindler. They have

Lacrosse sticks have evolved since the game was first played hundreds of years ago, but the basic design and function remains the same.

both played lacrosse since they were barely out of diapers. The Iroquois Nationals are the only Native American team allowed to compete internationally in any sport. The Federation of International Lacrosse (FIL) recognized the Iroquois Confederacy as a member country in 1990. That gave the Iroquois equal status with nations such as the United States, Canada, and Australia.

The FIL had 30 men's national lacrosse teams in 2010. The Iroquois Nationals were ranked fourth in the world. The Iroquois were ranked as high as number two in 2007. That is despite having just 125,000 Native American people from which they can draw players. The United States, on the other hand, has a population of more than 300 million.

Almost any Native American lacrosse player would be honored to play for the Iroquois Nationals. But the team is

'TIL DEATH DON'T WE PART

Like Brett Bucktooth's son, many Iroquois boys are given small lacrosse sticks at birth. Iroquois players keep their lacrosse sticks by their sides at all times. Some even bring theirs to bed with them at night. When Iroquois lacrosse players die, they are buried with their sticks. The Iroquois believe that the first thing you do after entering the spirit world is play a game of lacrosse with your ancestors, and so the deceased must have their sticks close.

Many Iroquois boys, like the ones pictured, still begin to play lacrosse at a young age.

made up mostly of athletes from the six tribes that make up the Iroquois Confederacy. They are the Onondaga, the Mohawk, the Oneida, the Cayuga, the Seneca, and the Tuscarora Nations.

Bucktooth and Schindler are members of the Onondaga Nation. They play lacrosse because their fathers and grandfathers and great-great-grandfathers played the sport and passed it on to them. "Lacrosse is something that has been played for centuries among our people," Bucktooth said. "There is a lot of pride that goes into this game." As Schindler put it, "Lacrosse here is a way of life."

Bucktooth and Schindler grew up on reservations. Lacrosse has helped them see the world outside of the reservations. Both went on to play for National Collegiate Athletics Association (NCAA) Division I universities. Today the sport allows them to travel throughout the world for competitions. But lacrosse also keeps them deeply connected to their tribe. It is a link to their ancestors and to the future generations of Native American lacrosse players.

Schindler is the grandson of an Onondaga chief. He was born and raised on the Onondaga Nation reservation in upstate New York. It is a 7,300-acre territory. The reservation is governed by its

THE LOST ART OF WOOD

Traditionally, Native American lacrosse sticks were made from wood. Most modern sticks are made from aluminum or other materials. But certain artisan lacrosse manufacturers like Alf E. Jacques still make sticks the old-fashioned way. Jacques selects the tree first hand. Then he steams, bends, and cures the wood for the Nationals defense sticks. The Iroquois believe their sticks are gifts from Mother Earth. They believe that the spirit of the tree from which they were made has been transferred to the Iroquois player.

Drew Bucktooth, *center*, playing for the Iroquois Nationals, cradles against Japan during the 1996 Under-19 World Lacrosse Championships.

own laws rather than those of the United States. His first name, Gewas (pronounced GAY-wass) means "clear as the sky." As a child, Schindler played lacrosse for tribal teams. However, his quick feet and masterful stick work earned him a place at Avon Old Farms. That is a prep school for top athletes in Connecticut. Schindler went on to play for Loyola University in Baltimore,

Maryland. There he was named an All-American in 1997, 1998, and 1999.

Similarly, Bucktooth started playing lacrosse when he was just three years old. He was a star lacrosse player at Lafayette High School in LaFayette, New York. Bucktooth scored 77 goals and recorded 41 assists during his senior year. He went on to play for Syracuse University in New York. Bucktooth earned All-American honors with Syracuse in 2005 and 2006.

Many Iroquois face a difficult choice. They can choose to live a traditional life on the reservation as their ancestors did. They can also choose to leave and pursue a career in the modern world. Schindler and Bucktooth have proved that Iroquois people can do both. The two play for the Nationals in the FIL and in the National Lacrosse League (NLL). The NLL is a professional indoor lacrosse league.

Schindler was a member of the NLL's New York Titans in 2007. He commuted 240 miles (386 km) from the Onondaga

SIMPLIFIED NAME

The Iroquois first referred to the sport now known as lacrosse as *Deyhontsigwa'ehs*, or "To bump hips." Deyhontsigwa'ehs was a means for Iroquois men to honor their Creator.

reservation to New York City for his games. The trip took him past Onondaga creek and the lacrosse fields of his childhood. At the end was the bustling metropolis that is New York City. But every time he left the reservation, Schindler always knew he would soon return to his home.

Schindler has worked hard for a successful life. Yet he has never abandoned the traditions and customs of his people. Despite his professional success, Schindler still plays in the Iroquois' sacred medicine game several times each year. The medicine game is closely related to lacrosse but is played to help heal the sick. As Brett Bucktooth's father Freeman Bucktooth said of the medicine game, "Whatever illness you have, it pushes it away. It's amazing how well it cures you."

For the Bucktooths, lacrosse skills seem to be inherited. Freeman Bucktooth has four sons who all play lacrosse. Brett and one of his brothers, Drew Bucktooth, played at Syracuse.

ACCESS DENIED

In the summer of 2010, the Iroquois Nationals were denied entry into England for the World Championships after the team attempted to travel using passports issued by the Iroquois Confederacy. The British government said the passports lacked security features and were too easy to duplicate. The British were willing to accept passports from Canada or the United States. But the Iroquois, who are fiercely proud of their heritage and of their independence from the countries that surround their reservations, wanted the UK officials to recognize them as a sovereign nation.

"We have been around for over 1,000 years," Nationals director Percy Abrams said. "We've certainly preempted the American government or Canadian government. We have a right to self-determination. We have a right to present our own passport." The British and the Iroquois could not reach an agreement, so the championships were played without the Nationals for the first time since 1989.

That is the same college for which their father played. Like Brett, Drew Bucktooth also plays for the Nationals as an attack. And their father, Freeman, is the Iroquois Nationals' offensive coach. "Lacrosse is a brotherhood," Brett Bucktooth said.

Whenever the Iroquois Nationals play abroad, people pay attention. The team serves as a sort of cultural ambassador for the Iroquois Confederacy, as well as for all other Native Americans. While overseas, the players spread the word about what life is really like for Native Americans in the United States. They dismiss myths people might have about Native Americans.

Lacrosse is one of the fastest growing sports in the world. The

Drew, *left*, and Brett Bucktooth, *right*, play on the Iroquois Nationals lacrosse team. Their father Freeman, *center*, is the team's offensive coach.

game is more than that for Schindler and Bucktooth and the rest of the Iroquois Nationals players. For them, lacrosse is a tradition, a means of success, a brotherhood, and a platform for communication. For them, lacrosse is more than just a sport. It's their identity.

CHAPTER 2

AMERICA'S FIRST SPORT

Native Americans have been playing stick-and-ball games since before recorded time. The Native American tribes played the sports for fun. They also played to celebrate births and deaths. They played to settle disputes between tribes. They even played as physical training for hunting and war.

Each tribe had its own version of the game now known as lacrosse. Native Americans living in the Great Lakes region used a stick with a wooden pocket to transport a small, deerskin ball to a goal. Tribes in the Southeast used two small sticks, one in each hand. And tribes in the Northeast and Canada played a version more similar to the modern game. They used a four- to five-foot (1.22- to 1.52-m) long stick with a string-laced pocket.

Different tribes played lacrosse with different rules that changed from game to game, sometimes allowing two sticks to be used instead of one.

European settlers first witnessed these Native American stickball games during the 1600s. The first settlers to write about these sports did not seem to fully understand just how important the games were to the Native Americans playing them.

Warriors in Training

For many Native tribes, lacrosse prepared young, inexperienced male warriors for battle. The Cherokee tribe even referred to the game as "little brother of war."

Early lacrosse games were played on fields that could be anywhere from 500 yards (457 m) to a half-mile (0.8 km) long. In some cases, the goals were several miles apart. Teams had hundreds to sometimes more than 1,000 players. There were no sidelines. That meant play would stretch north, south, east, and west in all directions. Games started at sunrise and ended at sundown. And they often lasted for two to three days each.

Despite these chaotic conditions, in 1721 a Jesuit missionary noted that the ball rarely touched the ground during games.

Many tribes would start a lacrosse game by clearing the fields of stone and debris. They often used hoes made from deer and moose antlers to do so. Fields were located close to the safety of the village. Goals could be a single tree, pole, or rock. In these games, once the ball hit the goal the team scored. For some tribes, however, the goal was made up of two posts standing six to nine feet (1.8 to 2.7 m) apart. A team would score by passing the ball between the posts. Teams would play to a set score. Once that score was reached, play stopped.

As in war, tackling, wrestling, tripping, charging, and striking opponents with the stick were allowed. Players did not have pads or helmets. And they often played barefoot, so injuries were expected and common. Games were played in the heat of the summer and in the dead of winter. The Sioux would even play on frozen lakes while wearing moccasins. Such an environment was ideal for developing strength and endurance in young males.

ONE BALL OR ANOTHER

Native American lacrosse balls came in two varieties. Solid balls were usually made of wood. And softer, more resilient balls were usually stuffed animal skins.

Players would often fast before games. They wanted to imitate the long periods of time warriors must go without food. The young men were allowed to eat at times. But they did not eat the meat of any animal considered to be weak or timid. Many players painted their bodies red and decorated themselves with feathers from hawks and eagles. They believed the accessories would give them better eyesight, precision, and speed.

Lacrosse as Religion

Many Native American sports were played to honor spirits and gods. Native Americans played games to change the weather and to ensure good harvests. For them, sports such as lacrosse were more than just recreation.

The Iroquois believe lacrosse was a gift to their people from their Creator. Several Algonquin tribes told stories about the Great Spirit revealing lacrosse to them through dreams. The

TENNIS ANYONE?

The first European accounts of Native American lacrosse often compared it to tennis. The settlers did not write much about how the natives handled their sticks, but historians believe early Native American sticks might have had springy, tight-knit webbing like that of a tennis racquet. They also think the ball might have been hit from player to player and not tossed or carried as it is today.

Some early lacrosse matches became large spectator events as the size of the teams swelled to hundreds of players on each side.

Abenaki believed aurora borealis, or the Northern Lights, was actually their ancestors playing lacrosse in the heavens.

Some tribes considered lacrosse sacred. They only played to cure the ill or honor a spirit. And almost all tribes believed the athletes on the field did not win the game. Rather, they believed it was won by the spirits and the forces guiding them.

Medicine men played important roles on lacrosse teams. The medicine men themselves did not play lacrosse. But their assistance was considered essential to success. Teams hired the best and most well known medicine men to ensure their team's victory using magical spells and potions. Sometimes they hired many medicine men.

Medicine men made lacrosse balls and gave them certain powers. For Cherokee medicine men, the skin for the balls' outside covers had to come from a squirrel that was killed but not shot. The Creek placed inchworms in the center of their lacrosse balls. They believed inchworms were invisible to birds. Therefore, they would make the ball invisible and hard for their competition to track.

Sticks received the same types of treatment. Native Americans adorned their lacrosse sticks with feathers. They also engraved them with snakeskin patterns. They believed their sticks would take on those animals' best attributes. Players would slip their sticks into sacred waters before games. They also would rub potions made by medicine men onto their sticks' strings, as well as onto their bodies. They believed it would make them stronger and more powerful.

Lacrosse is one of the oldest sports in the world. It was played in North America long before European settlers arrived.

Lacrosse was a key feature of Native American funeral and memorial services. Members of the Fox tribe would play to honor a deceased tribesman's spirit before it left the earth. The Menominee would play annual lacrosse matches to memorialize famous players. These games were mentioned in the settlers' first recordings of lacrosse. Some tribes still play the games today.

Over time, the European settlers began to understand how significant lacrosse was to the Native American tribes. They also saw how impressive the sport could be. The settlers started enforcing rules and modifying the tribes' style of play, eventually leading to the modern game.

CHAPTER 3

THE MODERN GAME TAKES SHAPE

E uropean settlers were not exactly quick to play lacrosse with Native American warriors. The first account of white settlers playing lacrosse came in the mid 1700s. That is when a group from the Mohawk tribe taught the sport to French-Canadians living in Montreal, Canada.

The lesson must not have gone well for the settlers. A full century passed before white men again attempted the sport. For many years, the general opinion in the United States and Canada was that no group of whites could ever match a Native American lacrosse team. But in 1851, more than 200 years after settlers first observed lacrosse, it happened. A team of white players in Montreal defeated a Native American team of the same size for the first time in recorded history.

The Columbia University lacrosse team practices in 1908. Ivy league schools such as Columbia helped lacrosse grow in the United States.

1867: A Big Year

The Dominion of Canada was created on July 1, 1867. Canada was commonly referred to by that name through the 1970s. Some claimed lacrosse was declared the new country's national sport. These reports proved false. But lacrosse still swept Canada that year. It branched out to other parts of the world, as well.

Montreal-born dentist William George Beers is often called the father of modern lacrosse. He formed the Canadian National Lacrosse Association in 1867. Canada had just eight lacrosse teams early in that year. By the end of the year, the country had 80 teams. Beers had played lacrosse since he was six years old. He drafted the first official set of rules for the sport. Many rules were similar to those of modern lacrosse. However, the changes added more structure to the Native American games.

Despite the new rules, Native Americans helped spread lacrosse overseas. In 1867, a Native American team visited England, Ireland, France, and Scotland. For the English, lacrosse was love at first sight. Clubs opened in Blackheath, Richmond, and Liverpool that year. And in 1868, the English Lacrosse Association (ELA) formed. The ELA was the first association to put a time limit on the game.

The United States Catches On

In 1867, another group of Native American players put on a lacrosse demonstration. This time they did it at the Saratoga Springs fairgrounds in New York. Later in the year, eight white US players challenged eight Canadian-Indian players in an exhibition match in Troy, New York. Soon after, the Mohawk Club of Troy formed. It was the United States' first lacrosse club. The Mohawk Club played four games in 1868. It lost all of them to Canadian teams. But lacrosse kept spreading as clubs popped up in the Midwest, North, and Eastern parts of the United States.

Beers took a club team and a group of Native American players to the British Isles in 1876. They played in front of Queen Victoria at Windsor Castle in England. According to reports, the Queen was quite pleased with what she saw. That same group then played at the elite and exclusive Westchester Polo Club in Newport, Rhode Island. More than 8,000 people showed up for the contest. *The New York Herald* reported the event was hugely successful. "The universal verdict is that

WE'RE NUMBER ONE

The Upper Canada College of Toronto formed a club lacrosse team in 1867. This was the first college to play lacrosse.

lacrosse is the most remarkable, versatile, and exciting of all games of ball," it said.

Lacrosse Goes to College

As lacrosse spread, US colleges got in on the action. In the fall of 1877, New York University (NYU) played Manhattan College. It was the United States' first intercollegiate lacrosse game. The United States National Amateur Lacrosse Association (USNALA) was founded in 1879. The original members included NYU and Harvard University as well as nine club teams.

The association was the creation of life-long lacrosse player John R. Flannery. At age 16, Flannery played for Montreal's Shamrock Club. Later he moved to Boston, Massachusetts. He helped organize the Union Lacrosse Club there. Later, while in New York, he joined the Ravenswood Club. His leadership and

TOUGH CROWD

New York City saw its first lacrosse match in 1868. The big city newspapers had mixed reviews of the sport. As the *New York World* put it, lacrosse was "the most exciting and at the same time the most laughter provoking among the whole range of outdoor sports." The *New York Tribune* called it "a madman's game, so wild it is." And the *Times* weighed in calling lacrosse "a noisy game and one of much excitement."

enthusiasm for lacrosse led to the formation of nine clubs in New York state alone. It also led to his title as the father of American lacrosse.

The USNALA sponsored the first intercollegiate tournament in 1881. Princeton University, Columbia University, Harvard, and NYU competed. Harvard beat Princeton to win the title. The Intercollegiate Lacrosse Association formed the following year. Those four schools joined along with Yale University and Johns Hopkins University. By 1900, dozens of colleges fielded lacrosse teams. Some were big colleges and some were small. All of these were men's teams, however. Organized women's lacrosse was still in its earliest stages.

Changes on the Quad

More college lacrosse players meant major innovations for the sport. In 1897, Stevens Institute of Technology captain Rossiter Scott fastened a tennis net to the back of the goal posts. That made it much easier to tell when the ball had actually passed through the posts. Scott passed the idea on to his friend Ronald Abercrombie at Johns Hopkins. Abercrombie and his teammates started using the new goals in 1898. Soon after, other colleges followed.

Abercrombie was short in stature. So he came up with another groundbreaking modification: he shortened his stick. Five- and six-foot (1.5- and 1.8-m) long sticks were standard for all players around the turn of the century. But Abercrombie and his teammates liked how much lighter and easier to handle the shorter sticks were for their attacks.

The Johns Hopkins attackers also switched to smaller nets. That meant smaller targets for their opponents. In addition, they shortened their goalkeepers' sticks. While their defenders still carried long sticks, they made those sticks lighter, as well. These changes enabled the Johns Hopkins players to maneuver better. That gave rise to the short passing game put into place by Johns Hopkins coach William H. Maddren. He spent five years at Johns Hopkins. During that time the team went 25–6 and won three national championships.

The heart of college men's lacrosse has remained in the United States' Northeast. Johns Hopkins, Harvard, Princeton, and Navy are all located in that region. They combined to win nearly 70 national titles from 1881 to 1971. That is when the National Collegiate Athletic Association (NCAA) took over the sport. As of 2011, Duke and North Carolina were the southern-most schools to win national championships in men's lacrosse.

Canada captain Paddy Brennan battles for the ball during an exhibition game at the 1908 Olympic Games in London. Canada won the gold medal.

Taking It to the Games

Lacrosse innovations continued into the new century as the sport garnered more international attention. The 1904 Olympic Games were in St. Louis, Missouri. There, lacrosse was played as an official Olympic event for the first time. The Shamrocks from Canada won the gold medal. The competition also included an indigenous Mohawk team from Canada known as the Mohawk Indians. One of their players had the unusual name of "Man Afraid Soap." The Canadians repeated in 1908 at the Olympic Games in London, England. However, that would be the last time lacrosse was played as an official Olympic sport.

Lacrosse was welcomed back into the Olympic Games in 1928 but only as an exhibition sport. That meant no medals were awarded. Johns Hopkins earned the right to represent the United States at the 1928 Games in Amsterdam, Netherlands. Johns Hopkins returned for the 1932 Games in Los Angeles, California. They beat the Canadian national team in two out of three Olympic exhibition matches. Today, Johns Hopkins is the home of US Lacrosse, the sport's national governing body. US Lacrosse started in June of 1959. Back then it was known as The Lacrosse Hall of Fame Foundation.

Lacrosse was last featured as a demonstration sport in the Olympic Games in 1948. An all-England team represented Great Britain. It played against Rensselaer Polytechnic Institute.

LACROSSE IN CHARM CITY

Teams from Maryland such as Johns Hopkins, Navy, Maryland, and St. John's have long dominated the college men's game. In the early 1900s, Baltimore had no professional sports teams. So the region instead focused on amateur lacrosse. By the 1920s, both of Baltimore's major public high schools and all of its private schools had lacrosse programs. The region produced winning coaches at Princeton and Army. The 1942 national champion Princeton team, coached by Johns Hopkins graduate Bill Logan, became the first northern team to beat all three Maryland Powers (Hopkins, Maryland, and Navy) in the same year. As former Princeton coach Bill Tierney, a former Johns Hopkins assistant, told a reporter in 1998, "Nowhere else will lacrosse ever have that history or that importance or carry the weight it does in Baltimore."

The school from New York represented the United States. The game was played at Wembley Stadium, near London. The final score was a 5–5 tie. In that era, there was no overtime played when games ended in a tie.

The Women's Game

Organized women's lacrosse got its start in the United Kingdom. In 1890, St. Leonards School in St. Andrews, Scotland, fielded the first girls' lacrosse teams. Jane Frances Dove was headmistress when lacrosse was introduced.

No other women played lacrosse at the time. So all the matches were between dorms at the school. Eventually, other high schools in the United Kingdom added teams. In 1912, the Ladies Lacrosse Association was formed with representation from England, Scotland, and Wales.

The United States, however, was slow to accept women's lacrosse. Having only seen the men's game, people assumed lacrosse was too violent and rough for women. Oddly enough, the sometimes-brutal sport of field hockey was widely played by US women. Many of lacrosse's earliest proponents in the United States were women's field hockey stars.

Lacrosse was introduced to women at Wellesley College in Massachusetts in 1890 with the help of the men's lacrosse team at nearby Harvard University. Cara Gascoigne was a physical education teacher from England. In 1914, she attempted to start a club for her students at Sweetbriar College. In both cases, the game failed to take hold.

Later, a demonstration game was organized at Wellesley in 1924. But it was not until the appointment of Joyce Cran Barry, another teacher from England, that the game was added to the physical education curriculum in the late 1920s.

Rosabelle Sinclair had attended St. Leonards School and was a former Scotland player. In 1926, she was the athletic director at Bryn Mawr School in Baltimore, Maryland. Sinclair introduced lacrosse to her students there. They played their first matches that year against other schools from Baltimore.

Women's lacrosse first gained popularity in Great Britain. Teams such as this one often traveled to the United States to play in exhibition games.

Over time, women's clubs started popping up in New York, New York; Philadelphia, Pennsylvania; Boston, Massachusetts; and throughout the Northeast. Enthusiasts such as Sinclair and Cran Barry helped this growth by writing and lecturing about the sport. They also ran yearly sports camps. Then, in 1931, the United States Women's Lacrosse Association (USWLA) was formed to govern the sport. Many people looked down upon women playing sports during that time. That meant women's lacrosse expanded at a slower rate than men's lacrosse. But it was expanding nonetheless.

CHAPTER 4

A NEW ERA

Although men's lacrosse was no longer in the Olympic Games, it continued to grow in popularity—especially in the United States. By 1926, colleges as far south as the University of Georgia were fielding men's lacrosse teams as members of the USILA.

Women's lacrosse continued to grow as well. Following World War II, England lacrosse captain Margaret Boyd started traveling up and down the US East Coast teaching clinics to women wherever she went. In 1971, she founded the International Federation of Women's Lacrosse Association (IFWLA). The IFWLA merged with the Federation of International Lacrosse (FIL), the men's international lacrosse association, to form the united FIL in 2008.

In 2011, 43 states had a championship tournament for boys' high school lacrosse and 35 had a girls' tournament.

AMERICA TUNES IN TO LACROSSE

In 1976, lacrosse found a national audience. Cornell and Maryland were back in the finals of the men's NCAA tournament that year. Football Hall of Famer Frank Gifford was there, as well. Gifford did play-by-play announcing for the game, which was shortened and broadcast on tape-delay for ABC's *Wide World of Sports*. Cornell won 16–13 in double overtime, and Gifford called the game "without question the most exciting sporting event I've ever seen."

Other big changes throughout the 1970s and 1980s led to huge gains in participation in women's lacrosse. In 1972, the US government passed legislation called Title IX. It required US schools and colleges to give equal opportunities to men and women in sports and other activities. The Association for Intercollegiate Athletics for Women (AIAW) originally organized women's college lacrosse. But in 1982, the more established NCAA took over. The NCAA still organizes men's and women's college lacrosse.

Today, more women than ever are playing the sport. In 2000, roughly 15,000 girls were playing high school lacrosse at 600 high schools across the country. By 2009, that number topped 90,000 with more than 2,400 high schools offering the sport. All told, 221,611 women were playing or coaching lacrosse in the United States in 2009.

Tourney Time

Cornell University's men's lacrosse team started its 1971 season with a heartbreaking 10–9 loss to Virginia. The Big Red from Cornell bounced back, though. They won their next 13 games in a row. Included in that run was the first NCAA championship game. Cornell beat Maryland 12–6 to claim the first NCAA men's lacrosse title.

Prior to 1971, the USILA's executive board had voted to decide the national champion based on regular-season records and the strength of each team's schedule. This resulted in 11 ties. Squads from three schools shared the Wingate Trophy, which was awarded to the collegiate men's champion, in 1967 and again in 1970. When the NCAA took over, it allowed teams to decide the champion in a national tournament. That resulted in one decisive champion. That year, eight teams were invited to play at Hofstra University in Hempstead, New York.

The AIAW organized the first women's collegiate lacrosse championships in 1978. Both the AIAW and the NCAA held tournaments in 1982 before the NCAA fully took over in 1983. Today, 16 teams earn invitations to the annual NCAA men's and women's tournaments. Both genders also now have three divisions of college lacrosse in which schools can play. Only

Division I and Division II can offer athletic scholarships. The biggest schools and best players generally play in Division I.

The NCAA tournament was just one of many major shake-ups to change the face of lacrosse during that time. Between the equipment, the dominant teams, and the style of play, lacrosse continued to innovate as it spread throughout the globe.

North America v. The World

As the game sped up, so did the players around the world. The first men's World Lacrosse Championships were held in 1967 in Toronto, Canada. The Mount Washington Lacrosse Club represented the United States. Australia and England also participated. The US team came out as champions with a 3–0 record. The tournament was held every four years after that. The US team only lost once until 2006.

In the mid- to late-1980s, the Iroquois Nationals joined these

WHAT AN UPSET!

The 1978 World Championships began with a round-robin format but added a final championship game. In its opening game, the United States ran away with a 28–4 victory over Canada. But Canada got its revenge in the championship. The Canadians pulled off what many consider to be one of the most stunning upsets in lacrosse history by beating the United States 17–16 in overtime. It was the first defeat for the United States in international competition in decades. And it would be the last until Canada finally regained the title in 2006.

four countries in the international competition. The Iroquois Nationals represented the Six Nation Iroquois Confederacy. In 1987, the Iroquois Nationals were given full member status. They participated in the 1990 World Championships in Perth, Australia.

The World Lacrosse Championships occur every four years. The FIL, which has been lacrosse's international governing body since 2008, organizes the event. The United States has advanced to the championship game in each of the first 11 tournaments. It won seven of the nine titles handed out from 1967 to 2010. Canada won the other two. Teams from 29 countries competed in the 2010 tournament, including Latvia, Japan, the Czech Republic, and South Korea.

The first Women's World Cup was played in 1982. In the final, the United States beat Australia 10–7. That was the same year that the NCAA took control of women's college lacrosse. The United States and Australia have remained the two dominant powers in international women's lacrosse. Through 2009, the United States had won six World Cup titles. Australia had won two. No other country had ever won the tournament. England was the only other country to ever qualify for the championship game, which it did twice.

Fresh Blood

Back in the men's college game, Johns Hopkins, Cornell, and Maryland owned the first 17 years of the NCAA tournament. They won a combined 12 championships. Johns Hopkins alone won seven. But in the late 1980s and into the 1990s, two new teams took control.

The Syracuse Orange burst onto the college scene. They went 15–0 and won the championship in 1988. The stars of that team were the creative twin brothers and future Lacrosse Hall of Famers Gary and Paul Gait. Gary Gait set records for scoring in a NCAA tournament game, in a single tournament, and in career tournaments. He went on to a storied career in the indoor NLL, where he became the league's all-time leading scorer. The Orange's victory in 1988 would be the first of three straight national titles for Syracuse and the Gaits. However, the Orange were forced to vacate their 1990 title. That was because the NCAA cited Paul Gait for being ineligible due to a rules violation. From 1988 to 2011, Syracuse took home nine national championships.

Another orange-clad team shared control of the NCAA trophy in the 1990s—Princeton. Under coach Bill Tierney, the Princeton Tigers won six titles from 1992 to 2001. Princeton's first three titles each came in overtime thrillers. Among them

Toby Price of Syracuse, *left*, and Jon Brothers of Maryland battle for a loose ball during the 1995 NCAA title game.

was a 10–9, double-overtime win against Syracuse in 1992. The rivals would meet in the championship game three straight times from 2000 to 2002. Princeton won again in 2001.

The 2000s saw a few new college names rise to the top, including Duke, Massachusetts, and Notre Dame. But many of the sport's longtime powerhouses remained dominant.

Women's Powers

Star attacker Candy Finn helped the Penn State Nittany Lions become the first dominant women's college lacrosse team. It won

Northwestern's Danielle Spencer races down the field during the 2010 NCAA title game against Maryland.

the AIAW title in 1978, 1979, and 1980. Finn was also a star field hockey player for the Nittany Lions.

Women's lacrosse continued to grow when the NCAA took over in 1982. But schools from the Northeast continued to dominate. The University of Maryland had played in the AIAW championship game four times between 1978 and 1982, winning the 1981 title. Upon joining the NCAA in 1983, the Maryland

Terrapins continued to be a top team. They reached the NCAA championship game seven times over the next 12 years and won it twice. Then, beginning in 1995, Maryland won an amazing seven titles in a row.

After many years of the sport being dominated by East Coast schools, a major change occurred during the early 2000s. In 2002, Northwestern University in Illinois reinstated its women's lacrosse program. Former Maryland star Kelly Amonte Hiller became the team's coach. Until then, Penn State had been the westernmost team to win the NCAA title. But starting in 2005, the Northwestern Wildcats won five in a row. The Wildcats nearly won six, but they lost to Maryland in the 2010 NCAA championship game. The two teams met again in the 2011 NCAA championship game.

AIR GAIT

Anyone who watched the 1988 NCAA semifinal game between Syracuse and the University of Pennsylvania remembers at least one thing: the birth of Air Gait. Syracuse attacker Gary Gait, who learned the move while playing indoor lacrosse in his native Canada, rushed from behind the net, jumped over the cage of the goal and, while suspended in mid air, fired a shot past the stunned Penn keeper. The move looked something like basketball great Michael Jordan's classic "Air Jordan" pose. And that is how it was named. Gait unleashed the breathtaking display twice in that game.

Pennsylvania coach Tony Seaman asked to see a replay following his team's 11–10 loss. He said he had never seen anything like it in his 22 years of coaching. Gait's goals were ruled fair at the time, but the NCAA would later forbid such diving shots both in front of and behind the goal.

Northwestern avenged the previous season's loss to win its sixth title in seven years.

Going Pro

For many years, the top men could play for their national teams after college, but there were not opportunities to play professionally. But as collegiate men's lacrosse continued to grow in popularity during the late 1990s, the demand for a professional league grew. In 2001, Major League Lacrosse (MLL) debuted as just that.

In 2011, the MLL had six teams throughout the United States and Canada. Except for the Denver Outlaws, all of the teams were in the Eastern Time Zone. The league is the professional home to approximately 230 of the world's top men's lacrosse players. Since 2003, the ESPN network has been broadcasting MLL games live to a national audience.

The MLL might be the most high profile men's lacrosse league, but it is not the only one. The Eagle Pro Box Lacrosse League began in 1986 as an indoor lacrosse league. Indoor lacrosse, also known as box lacrosse, is popular on many Native American reservations and in Canada where cold weather forces people inside for much of the year. Each team fields six players

Gary Gait retired in 2011 as the NLL's second all-time points leader with 1,165. Many consider him to be one of the best lacrosse players ever.

on a surface that resembles a hockey rink—minus the ice, of course. Box lacrosse games are known for their exciting action on their smaller, enclosed fields. With constant action and lots of contact, box lacrosse is similar to ice hockey.

After several teams came and went, the league became known by its current name, the NLL, in 1998. At its peak, the NLL had 13 teams. In 2011, it had 10 teams throughout the United States and Canada. Although some of the teams play in fancy National Hockey League arenas, the NLL is considered a minor league. Many of the players work full-time jobs during the day before playing lacrosse on nights and weekends.

Lacrosse in the Twenty-First Century

Lacrosse has continued to grow in the United States and around the world. In 2009, more than 568,000 people were playing or coaching lacrosse in the United States. That was more than twice as many as in 2001. Over the next decade, colleges in all parts of the country began offering lacrosse.

During this time, record numbers turned out to watch the NCAA men's lacrosse tournaments. In 2003, the NCAA finals were played at M&T Bank Stadium. That is the home of the National Football League's Baltimore Ravens. It was the first time the finals were hosted outside of a university. A record crowd of 37,944 people showed up that year to watch Virginia beat Johns Hopkins 9–7. The game was broadcast live on ESPN. A record crowd of 9,782 fans showed up for the 2010 NCAA women's championship, in which Maryland beat Northwestern 13–10.

Attendance numbers for men peaked in 2008 when 48,970 people turned out to watch Syracuse defeat Johns Hopkins 13–10

Princeton's Jeff Froccaro, *left*, and Brown's Seth Ratner battle to win a face-off during a 2010 game.

for the championship. Some of those fans were likely there to see Paul Rabil play. That game was the last collegiate contest for the Johns Hopkins senior. Many consider him to be the first lacrosse superstar.

CHAPTER **5**

A SUPERSTAR IS BORN

Paul Rabil graduated from Johns Hopkins University in 2008. At the time, lacrosse was growing but it did not have an identifiable superstar. That was where Rabil stepped in.

At 6-foot-3-inches tall and weighing in at 220 pounds, Rabil looked more like a football linebacker than a lacrosse midfielder. In addition, he could shoot a lacrosse ball at 111 miles per hour—world-record speed. That is faster than a slap shot in hockey and almost as fast as an archer's arrow flies after it is sprung from a bow. At Johns Hopkins, Rabil won two NCAA Division I championships. He also was a four-time All-American. After graduation, Rabil signed with two professional lacrosse teams: the Boston Cannons of the outdoor MLL and the Washington Stealth of the indoor NLL. Rabil also broke many lacrosse

Paul Rabil of the Boston Cannons takes the field for an MLL game.

stereotypes. With long, shaggy hair and a nonchalant, laid-back style, Rabil separated himself from the privileged, buttoned-down image associated with the sport and its Ivy League roots.

Humble Beginnings

Rabil's mother was an art teacher and his father was a salesman. He grew up in the Maryland suburbs where he excelled at basketball and soccer. Rabil did not pick up a lacrosse stick until he was in middle school. But once he did, he was addicted. Early on, however, Rabil was not very good. As he put it, "I was bigger, faster, and stronger than my classmates, but they had better stick skills so they were better at lacrosse."

Not used to struggling in a sport, Rabil was determined to improve. He poured countless hours into lacrosse drills, conditioning, and strength training. He mastered the art of cradling the ball. He learned how to catch, throw, and shoot.

CRADLING

A lacrosse stick's net isn't all that roomy. To keep the ball in the net while running at full speed, cradling is essential. To cradle a ball, a player must rock or swing his stick back and forth. This creates centrifugal forces that push the ball deep into the pocket where it is more secure. Since women's lacrosse is less physical than men's, the women's basket is not as deep. That makes it even easier for the ball to fall out if a player is not properly cradling.

In 2005, freshman Paul Rabil led Johns Hopkins to its first national championship in 18 years.

And he did all of this while running at full speed with defenders trying to knock the ball away at every turn. "The more hours I put into getting better, the more passionate I was about making this sport my career," Rabil said.

Rabil was also a good student at Johns Hopkins. While playing for the Johns Hopkins Blue Jays, he maintained a 3.5 grade-point average. And he graduated with honors.

The Fruits of His Labor

Rabil joined the MLL and NLL in 2008. That same year, *Inside Lacrosse* fans voted him their player of the year. *Lacrosse*

Magazine awarded Rabil its Player of the Year honor in 2009. That was after he was named the MLL's Most Valuable Player (MVP) for leading the league in scoring with 53 points that season. It was the first time a midfielder was named the MLL MVP.

In 2010, Rabil led the Washington Stealth to a NLL title. At the World Lacrosse Championships in England that summer, he also helped Team USA win the gold medal back from Canada. Moreover, he nabbed the event's MVP crown. Boston Cannons coach Bill Daye, who coached Rabil in MLL, called the player "a freak of an athlete." Daye added, "He's strong, fast, and can stop or change directions on a dime."

The Face of Lacrosse

Before Rabil, most lacrosse manufacturers used generic, nameless athletes in their advertisements. But Rabil's popularity led companies to feature Rabil prominently in their ad campaigns. Rabil was even featured on nationally televised commercials that appeared on ESPN.

For Rabil, big-name sponsors meant he could make a living just playing lacrosse. With limited salaries, most professional lacrosse players also had to have full-time jobs. In 2010,

Rabil's Cannons teammates included salesmen, lawyers, and stockbrokers. As a full-time lacrosse player, Rabil would attend photo shoots, sign autographs, and make appearances for his sponsors. All of this helped elevate lacrosse and introduce it to new audiences.

Jen Adams

Women's lacrosse has rapidly grown in popularity since the NCAA took over the collegiate game in 1982. During that time, no woman has starred more than attacker Jen Adams. After growing up in Brighton, South Australia, Adams joined the University of Maryland lacrosse team in the midst of its seven straight NCAA titles.

Adams won an NCAA title with Maryland in each of her four years there, from 1998 to 2001. She was named National Player of the Year during three of those seasons. In 2001, Adams became the first recipient of the Tewaaraton Trophy, which is given to the nation's top player. Her 178 career assists and 445

Jen Adams of the University of Maryland led her team to four straight national titles from 1998 to 2001.

career points are both NCAA records. Adams also holds several Maryland records including career goals, assists, and points.

Before and after starring for Maryland, Adams was also a superstar for Australia. She first joined Australia's Under-19 team when she was 14 years old. Adams later led Australia to the 2005 Women's World Cup title with a 14–7 defeat over Team USA in the championship game. Her 26 assists and 47 total points in the tournament were the most of any player. In 2009, Adams again led all players with 26 assists and 41 points at that year's World Cup. Her team finished second to the United States that year.

Adams, who also won awards for her excellence in the classroom, has since turned her focus to coaching. She earned her first head coaching job when she took over the women's team at Loyola University in Maryland in 2009.

"It's bittersweet because I love Maryland so much, but at this point in my career it is time for me to make a difference at Loyola," Adams said at the time. "It is a very exciting time in my career and something that I am looking forward to taking on."

More Stars

Rabil and Adams are far from the only modern stars of lacrosse. Casey Powell scored a national record 292 goals with 261 assists while in high school. He did not slow down when he played for Syracuse and later in MLL. Through 2010, Powell was the MLL's all-time points leader. He was named to *Lacrosse Magazine's* All-Century team in 2000.

JIM BROWN

In 2002 the *Sporting News* named professional football Hall of Famer Jim Brown the greatest professional football player of all time, but some claim lacrosse was actually the former running back's best sport. Brown lettered in four sports, including lacrosse and football, before graduating from Syracuse in 1957. During his senior lacrosse season with Syracuse, he finished second in the nation in scoring and was named a first team All-American. Brown was quoted as having said, "I'd rather play lacrosse six days a week and football on the seventh."

Ned Crotty led his Duke team to the 2010 NCAA championship. In the semifinal, he assisted the game-winning goal with just 12 seconds left. Crotty was the top pick in the MLL draft that year. He also starred for the United States at the World Lacrosse Championships. Team USA was trailing Canada 10–9 going into the final minutes of the championship game. Then Crotty scored back-to-back goals to put the US squad in the lead en route to a 12–10 victory.

On the defensive side, few can match Canada's Brodie Merrill. He was named the MLL's Defensive Player of the Year every year from 2006 to 2010. He was also named the top defenseman at the 2010 World Lacrosse Championships.

Kristin Kjellman led her Northwestern Wildcats to NCAA titles in 2005, 2006, and 2007. She was named National Midfielder of the Year three times. And through 2011, Kjellman owns the all-time Northwestern record for goals (250). Kjellman won back-to-back Tewaaraton Trophies in 2006 and 2007. Only Northwestern attacker Hannah Nielson has matched that feat. The Australian playmaker won the trophy in 2008 and 2009. Nielson finished her career with a school-best 398 points. She also helped guide Northwestern to four NCAA championships.

Maryland's Caitlyn McFadden, *left*, scores over Syracuse goalie Liz Hogan during the second half of a 2010 NCAA tournament game.

Another women's lacrosse star quickly emerged after Kjellman and Nielson graduated. But Caitlyn McFadden did not play for Northwestern. The 2010 Tewaaraton Award winner starred for Maryland. She finished her career by helping Maryland end Northwestern's run of five straight NCAA titles with a 13–11 win in the 2010 title game.

Lacrosse is called the fastest sport on two feet. It is also one of the fastest growing sports in the United States and the world. With new lacrosse stars ready to grab the spotlight, and with lacrosse legends dating back hundreds of years, America's oldest sport should only continue to improve with age.

TIMELINE

1636 — Jesuit missionary Jean de Brebeuf first uses the term "la crosse" to describe the stick and ball games he saw the Huron tribe playing in Ontario, Canada.

1794 — A game between the Seneca and the Mohawk tribes leads to the creation of basic rules. Teams were limited to 60 men, playing fields took on a certain size, and goals were placed 500 yards apart.

1867 — William George Beers, a Montreal-based dentist and lifelong lacrosse player, forms the Canadian National Lacrosse Association, cementing his title as the father of modern lacrosse. Thanks to Beers's efforts, 72 new Canadian lacrosse clubs are established by the end of the year. Beers drafts the first official set of rules for the game.

1877 — New York University plays Manhattan College in the sport's first intercollegiate game. By the time the game was called for darkness, NYU led 2–0.

1879 — John R. Flannery earns the title "father of American lacrosse" by helping to form the USNALA.

1890 — The first women's lacrosse game is played at St. Leonards School in St. Andrews, Scotland. Teams consist of eight players.

1904 — Lacrosse is played as an Olympic sport at the Games in St. Louis, Missouri, and Canada wins the gold medal. Lacrosse is also a medal sport at the 1908 Games.

1913 — The first women's international matches are played in London, England, between England, Scotland, and Wales. Teams now consist of 12 players.

1931 — The USWLA is formed as the governing body for women's lacrosse. It holds the first national tournament in Greenwich, Connecticut, two years later.

1967	Coach Willis Bilderback of Navy wins his eighth straight intercollegiate title. Navy shared the title with Maryland and Johns Hopkins that year.
1971	The NCAA takes over men's college lacrosse and institutes the first national championship tournament, where Cornell University wins the inaugural title. The IFWLA is founded.
1982	Trenton State College hosts the first NCAA women's lacrosse national championship game, losing to the University of Massachusetts.
1987	The first formation of NLL, then known as the Eagle Pro Box Lacrosse League, brings box lacrosse teams to four US cities.
1995	The University of Maryland women's team wins its first of seven straight NCAA championships.
1998	US Lacrosse is founded as the national governing body for the men's and women's sport.
2001	MLL debuts as a professional league for field lacrosse.
2005	Northwestern University wins the women's NCAA Division I title, becoming the first team outside of the Eastern Time Zone to win a college lacrosse championship at any level.
2006	The men's World Championships are played in Ontario, Canada. The Canadians defeat the United States 15–10 in the gold-medal game. That snaps the Americans' 38-game winning streak that dated back to 1978.
2008	The men's and women's international lacrosse associations merge to form the FIL.
2010	At the men's World Lacrosse Championships, a record 29 countries turn out for the competition in Manchester, England. The Iroquois Nationals are denied access due to a dispute with their passports. The US reclaims the title thanks to a 12-10 win over Canada in the championship game.

LEGENDS OF LACROSSE

MEN

Scott S. Bacigalupo
Princeton and USA

Jim Brown
Syracuse and USA

Mike French
Cornell and Canada

Gary Gait
Syracuse and Canada

Paul Gait
Syracuse and Canada

Oren Lyons
Syracuse and USA

Dave Pietramala
Johns Hopkins and USA

Casey Powell
Syracuse and USA

Ryan Powell
Syracuse and USA

Leroy Shenandoah
Onondaga Tribe

Doug Turnbull
Johns Hopkins and USA

Jack Turnbull
Johns Hopkins and USA

WOMEN

Jen Adams
Maryland and Australia

Jane Diamond Barbieri
USA

Danielle Gallagher
William and Mary
and USA

Cherie Greer
Virginia and USA

Valerie Houston
Scotland

Vivian Jones
Wales

Kristin Kjellman
Northwestern and USA

Cheryl MacNeill
Canada

Sue Mellis Sofarnos
Australia

GLOSSARY

All-America
An honorary sports team made up of the best athletes in any given sport in a season. Players named to the All-America teams are called All-Americans.

assist
A pass that leads directly to a goal.

attendance
The number of fans who attend a game, a season, or a tournament.

cradle
To safely carry the ball in the stick's pocket by rocking or swinging the stick back and forth.

draft
The process by which professional teams acquire amateur players.

exhibition
A game played for fun with no implications for the winner or loser.

Jesuit
A religious order of priests in the Catholic Church. Jesuit missionaries were known for keeping detailed diaries with thorough descriptions of their surroundings.

medicine man
In Native American tribes, a person believed to have the power to heal and to see into the future.

missionary
A person sent on a religious mission, especially missions to promote Christianity in foreign countries.

pocket
The area of a lacrosse stick that carries the ball.

points
Goals and assists.

round robin
A tournament format in which each team plays every other team.

FOR MORE INFORMATION

Selected Bibliography

Fisher, Donald. Lacrosse: *A History of the Game*. Baltimore: The Johns Hopkins University Press, 2002. Print.

Pietramala, David and Neil Grauer. *Lacrosse: Technique and Tradition*. Baltimore: The Johns Hopkins University Press, 2006. Print.

Swissler, Becky. *Winning Lacrosse For Girls*. New York: Mountain Lion, 2004. Print.

Vennum Jr., Thomas. *American Indian Lacrosse: Little Brother of War*. Washington: Smithsonian Institution Press, 1994. Print.

Further Readings

Bruchac, Joseph. *The Warriors*. Plain City, OH: Darby Creek Publishing, 2003. Print.

Hoyt-Goldsmith, Diane. Lacrosse: *The National Game of the Iroquois*. New York: Holiday House, 1998. Print.

Philion, Michael. *Baggataway*. Bloomington, IN: Wordclay, 2009. Print.

Silverman, Chip. *Lucky Everyday: 20 Unforgettable Lessons from a Coach Who Made a Difference*. New York: Warner Books, 2004. Print.

Web Links

To learn more about lacrosse, visit ABDO Publishing Company online at **www.abdopublishing.com**. Web sites about lacrosse are featured on our Book Links page. These links are routinely monitored and updated to provide the most current information available.

Place to Visit

The US Lacrosse Museum & National Hall of Fame

113 W. University Parkway
Baltimore, MD 21210
410-235-6882, ext. 122
http://www.uslacrosse.org/museum/halloffame.phtml

This museum and hall of fame honors the history of lacrosse along with its greatest players and contributors. Artifacts, memorabilia, and art spanning from the Native American origins of lacrosse through today are featured. The Hall of Fame Gallery has interactive information about the hall of famers who have had the greatest impact on the sport. The museum also features a multimedia show and a documentary about lacrosse. Located in Baltimore, perhaps the sport's most enthusiastic city, the hall of fame is close to several high school, college, and professional lacrosse teams.

INDEX

About the Author

Annabelle Tometich is a journalist and author based in Southwest Florida. She writes about sports, food, and restaurants as a staff writer for *The News-Press*. She is a two-time Associated Press Sports Editors award winner and a proud University of Florida graduate. Tometich lives in Fort Myers, Florida, with her husband and her young son.